PICASSO
In His Words

Edited by Hiro Clark

CollinsPublishersSanFrancisco

A Division of HarperCollins*Publishers*

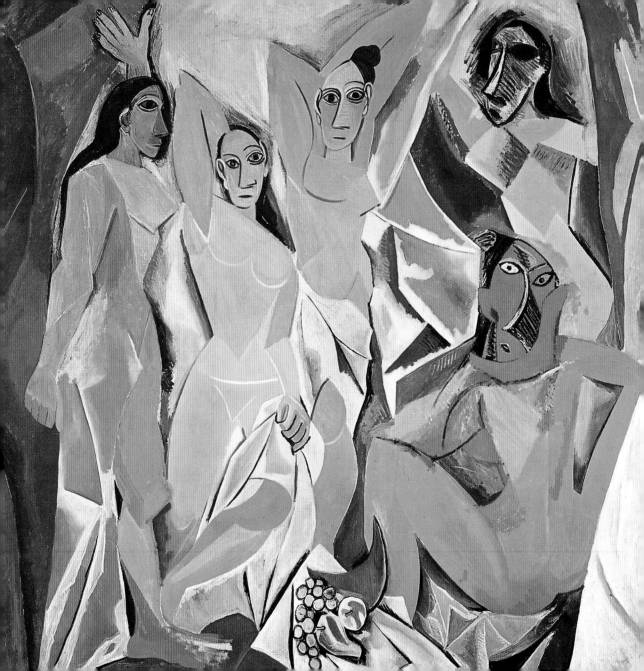

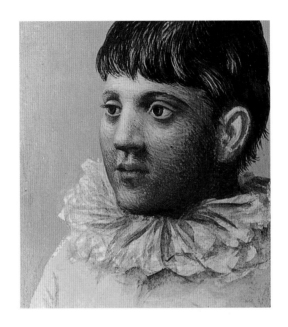

When I was a child, my mother said to me, "If you become a soldier you'll be a general. If you become a monk you'll end up as the Pope."

Instead, I became a painter and wound up as Picasso.

Designed by Gregory Wakabayashi
Produced by Welcome Enterprises, Inc., New York

First published in 1993 by Collins Publishers San Francisco,
1160 Battery Street, San Francisco, California 94111

Library of Congress Cataloging-in-Publication Data
Picasso, Pablo, 1881-1973.
Picasso : in his words / edited by Hiro Clark. 1st ed.
p. cm.
ISBN 0-00-255152-7
1. Picasso, Pablo, 1881-1973--Philosophy. I. Clark, Hiro.
II. Title.
ND553.P5A2 1993
760'.092--dc20   92-35162
                                  CIP

Special thanks to Lena Tabori, Dr. Theodore H. Feder,
and John Hanley.

Printed in Singapore by Toppan Printing Co., Inc.
10 9 8 7 6 5 4 3 2 1

Grateful acknowledgment is made for the following
sources:

Life With Picasso, by Françoise Gilot and Carlton Lake,
McGraw-Hill, Inc., New York. Copyright © 1964 McGraw-
Hill, Inc. Reprinted by permission of the publisher.

Matisse, Picasso, Miró: As I Knew Them, by Rosamond
Bernier, Alfred A. Knopf, Inc., New York. Copyright © 1991
Rosamond Bernier.

My Galleries and Painters, by Daniel-Henry Kahnweiler with
Francis Crémieux, The Viking Press, New York, 1971.
Copyright © 1971 Thames and Hudson Ltd.

Picasso: An Intimate Portrait, by Jaime Sabartés, Prentice
Hall, Inc., New York, 1948.

Picasso & Company, by Brassaï, Doubleday & Company, Inc.,
New York, 1966. Copyright © 1964 Editions Gallimard.

Picasso: Fifty Years of His Art, by Alfred H. Barr, Jr., The
Museum of Modern Art, New York. Copyright © 1946 The
Museum of Modern Art. Copyright renewed 1974. Reprinted
by permission of the publisher.

Picasso, His Life and Work, 3rd edition, by Roland Penrose,
University of California Press, Berkeley. Copyright © 1981
Roland Penrose.

Picasso Plain, by Hélène Parmelin, St. Martin's Press, New
York, 1963.

Picasso Says, by Hélène Parmelin, George Allen and Unwin
LTD, London, 1969.

Picasso: Women, by Hélène Parmelin, Harry N. Abrams, Inc.,
New York, 1964. All rights reserved.

Sunshine at Midnight: Memories of Picasso and Cocteau, by
Geneviéve Laporte, Macmillan Publishing, Co., Inc., New
York. Copyright © 1975 Douglas Cooper and Weidenfeld &
Nicolson. Reprinted by permission of Weidenfeld & Nicolson
Limited, London.

The Eye of Picasso, introduction by Roland Penrose, The New
American Library, New York, 1967.

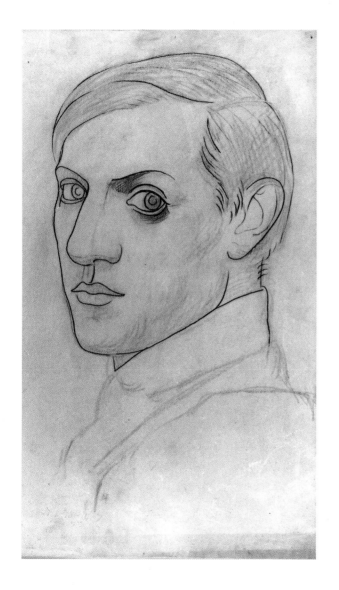

C O N T E N T S

INTRODUCTION 6

HIS WORDS 8

NOTES 92

LIST OF PLATES 94

INTRODUCTION

*P*icasso would have laughed, I suspect, at the idea of putting his words down in a book, completely divorced from the context in which they had been spoken, and thus cut off from their original meaning. It was the moment of creation that mattered most to him, and not what came after, or even before. One could not anticipate what was to be done or dwell on what had been done; one simply had *to do*. This is the path Picasso followed. He worked tirelessly throughout his life, immersed in the fullest, most open expression of his thoughts and ideas.

The status of Pablo Picasso (1881-1973) as the greatest artist of the twentieth century is well established. His name alone can evoke a parade of the most startling images the world has ever seen—*Les Demoiselles d'Avignon* (1907), *Still Life with Chair Caning* (1912), and *Guernica* (1937), to name a few. But tributes to Picasso, like frames around paintings, are mere decoration. It is the work itself which should command our attention. "If you want to kill a picture," Picasso once said, "all you have to do is to hang it beautifully on a nail and soon you will see nothing of it but the frame."

Though Picasso's art, in its great variety and abundance, has become well known to the world, his words—on the subjects of art, life, and love—are less familiar. He was not given to putting his ideas down in writing or to recording them on film or tape. It was left to his friends, lovers, and colleagues to preserve his words. And these words are so emblematic of the artist's nature that, in recording them for posterity, much of his essence has been retained.

Hélène Parmelin, a close friend whose reminiscences of the artist are among the most revealing, wrote: "There is no one more direct in his talk than Picasso, more natural both in words and in ideas, more in the habit of making spontaneous associations and unexpected but obvious comparisons, or more lapidary in his judgments. His conversation fizzes, attacks, adventures from idea to idea, from word to word; he digs deep, finds treasure, astonishes himself, or abandons the whole thing."

Parmelin described what one heard

6

when Picasso spoke—not necessarily the words themselves but the dynamic activity underlying the movement of his thoughts: "Picasso taught us . . . that there were no special barriers between ideas and words, and that the reason and the imagination when in full gallop know no limits but the fields of reality in which painting has been propagating itself for twenty-five thousand years."

The people whose recollections are presented here include, in addition to Mme Parmelin, others who figured prominently in Picasso's life, such as the poet Jaime Sabartés, a boyhood friend and his personal secretary for many years; Christian Zervos, a friend and critic who recorded some of Picasso's most significant statements on the subject of art and also assembled a thirty-three volume retrospective of his entire oeuvre; Roland Penrose, a close friend and the author of numerous books and essays about Picasso; Brassaï (Gyula Halász), the celebrated photographer who frequented his studio; and Françoise Gilot, who, for a time, shared the artist's life.

What these people possess in common is the experience of having known Picasso. If their collective memory does not always agree with itself, that is in keeping with the artist's own nature. As Parmelin observed, "the best method of approach to the truth of Picasso is perhaps to show to what extent he is always both the thing and its contrary. It is the most salient of his characteristics, [his] most immediately perceptible trait."

Picasso's uncompromising vitality was the definitive message of his life and is the legacy of his art. In capturing his words and setting them opposite his paintings, drawings, and lithographs, it is hoped that some measure of this vitality may be distilled. To fix Picasso in our minds once and for all, even if such a thing could be done, is beside the point. What matters is that in attempting to grasp the spirit of the man, we learn to confront our own fears and desires with a similar sense of passionate wonder. This is Picasso's challenge to those of us who would take life and nail it to the wall.

—H.C.

7

*E*veryone wants to understand
art. Why not try to understand the
songs of a bird? Why does one
love the night, flowers, everything
around one, without trying to
understand them? But in the case
of a painting people have to
understand. If only they would
realize above all that an artist
works of necessity, that he himself
is only a trifling bit of the world,
and that no more importance
should be attached to him than
to plenty of other things which
please us in the world, though
we can't explain them.

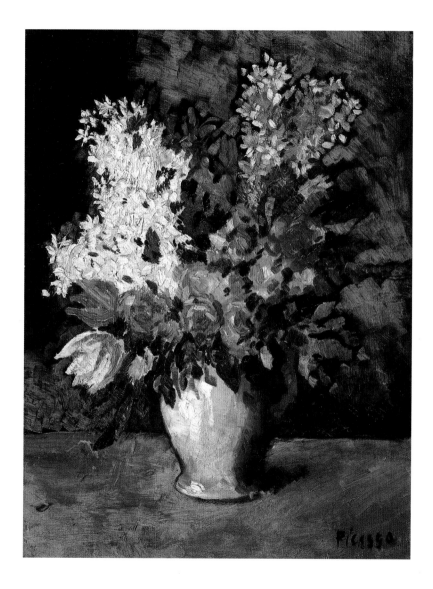

9

10

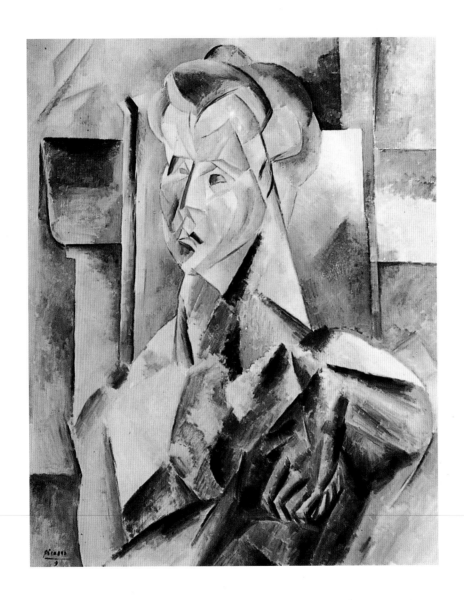

14

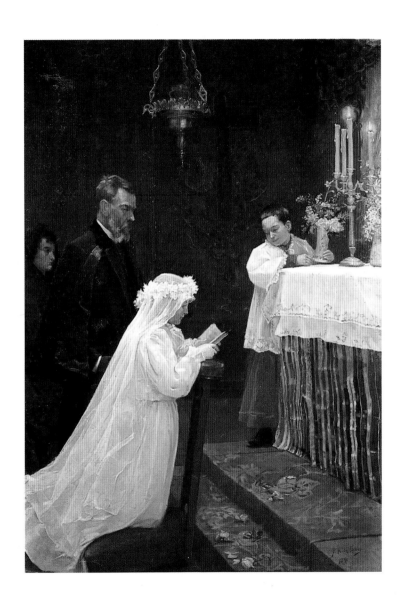

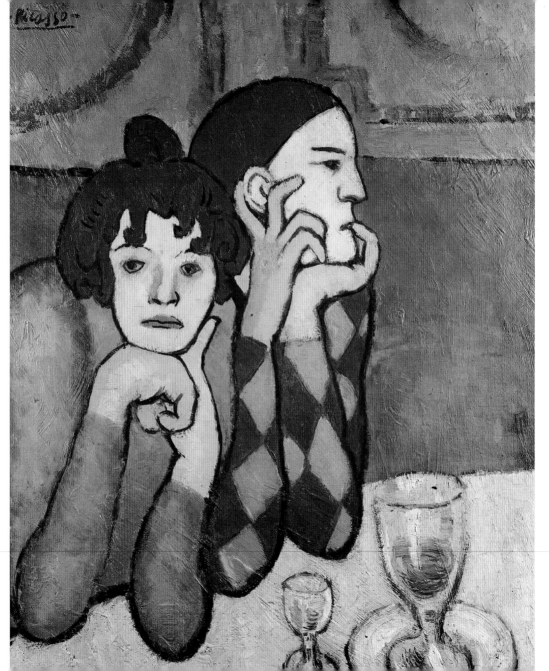

13

A picture is not thought out and settled beforehand. While it is being done it changes as one's thoughts change. And when it is finished, it still goes on changing, according to the state of mind of whoever is looking at it. A picture lives a life like a living creature,

undergoing the changes imposed on us by our life from day to day. This is natural enough, as the picture lives only through the man who is looking at it.

*P*ainting isn't an aesthetic operation;
it's a form of magic designed as a mediator
between this strange, hostile world and us,
a way of seizing the power by giving form
to our terrors as well as our desires.

When I came to that realization, I knew
I had found my way.

When I hear people speak of the evolution of an artist, it seems to me that they are considering him standing between two mirrors that face each other and reproduce his image an infinite number of times, and that they contemplate the successive images of one mirror as his past, and the images of the other mirror as his future, while his real image is taken as his present. They do not consider that they are all the same images in different planes.

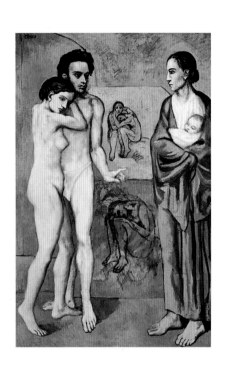

15

We all know that Art

is not truth. Art is a lie that

makes us realize truth,

at least the truth that is given

us to understand. The artist

must know the manner

whereby to convince others

of the truthfulness of his lies.

If he only shows in his work

that he has searched, and

re-searched, for the way to

put over lies, he would never

accomplish anything.

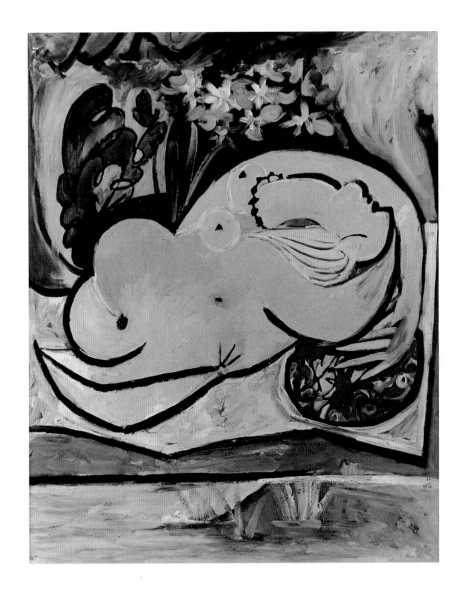

17

18

*T*he important thing is to do,
and nothing else; be what it may.

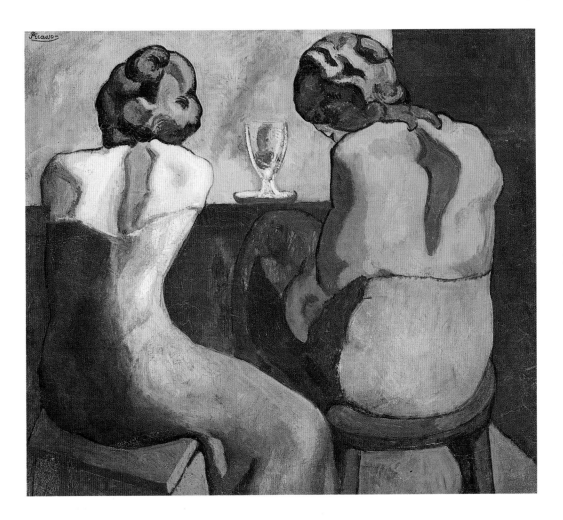

19

*S*o then, my dear sir, you are among
those who appreciate laurel leaves better
in a stew than on a crown?

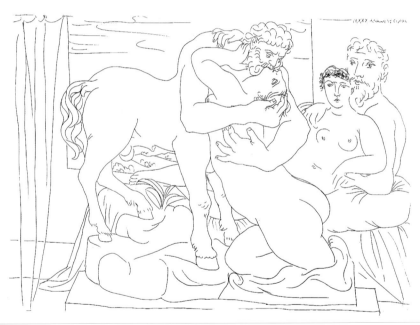

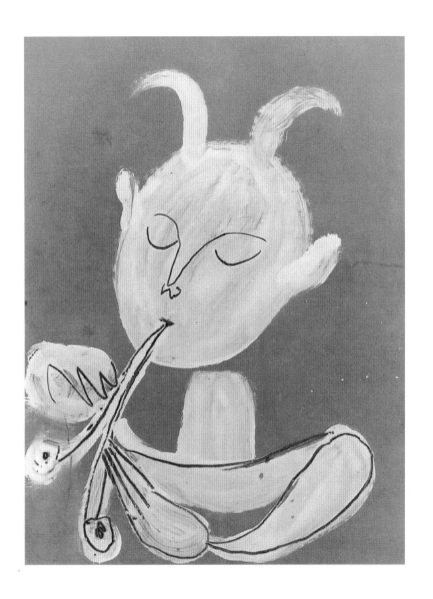

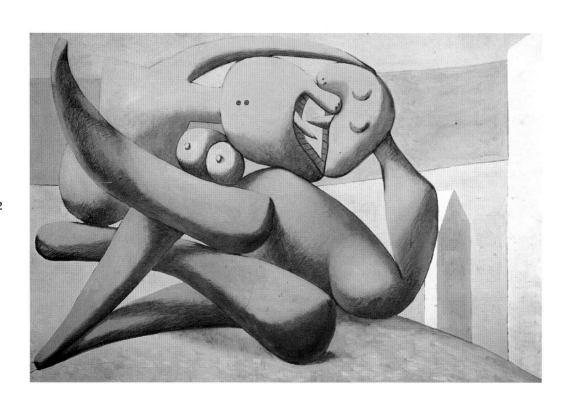

22

*E*verything exists in limited quantity—especially happiness. If a love is to come into being, it is all written down somewhere, and also its duration and content. If you could arrive at a complete intensity the first day, it would be ended the first day.

*I*f the things I really love—water, the sun, love—could be bought, I'd have been ruined long ago.

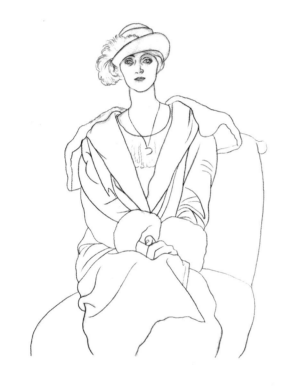

*I*f you know exactly

what you are going to do,

what's the good of doing it?

There's no interest in

something you know

already. It's much better

to do something else.

I never calculate. That's why the others who do,
calculate so much less accurately than I do.

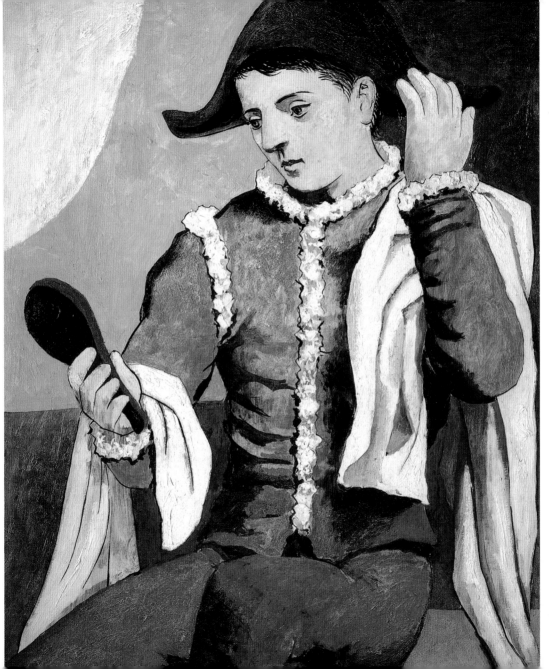

*F*reedom is something you have to
be very careful about. Whatever you do
you find yourself in chains. The freedom
not to do something means that you're
absolutely bound to do something else.

And there are your chains.

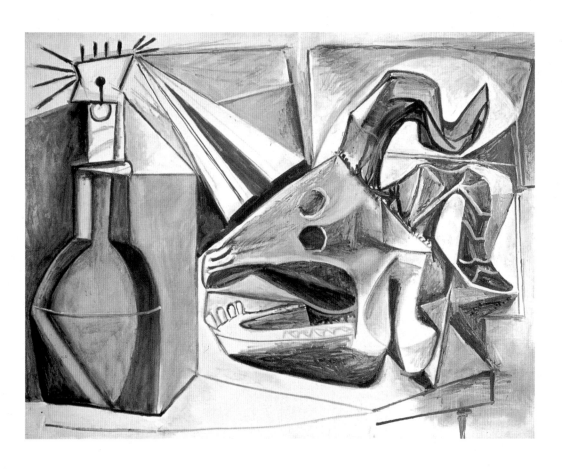

28

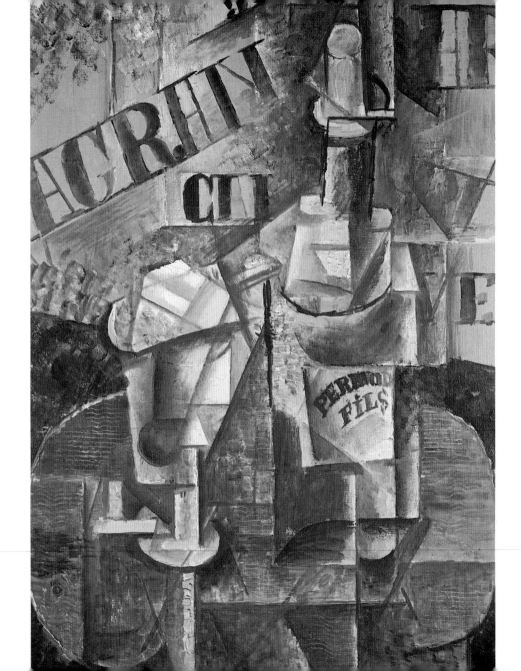

What is sculpture? What is painting? Everyone clings to old-fashioned ideas and outworn definitions, as if it were not precisely the role of the artist to provide new ones.

Anything new, anything worth doing, can't be recognized.

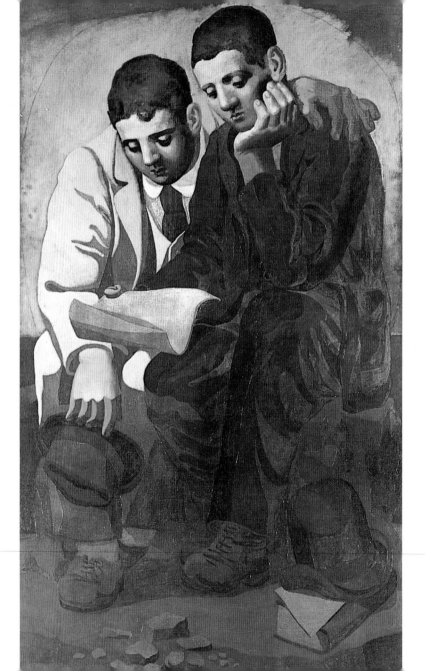

30

*I*can hardly understand the importance given to the word

research in connection with modern painting. In my opinion

to search means nothing in painting. To find, is the

thing. Nobody is interested in following

a man who, with his eyes fixed on the

ground, spends his life looking for the

pocketbook that fortune should put in

his path. The one who finds something

no matter what it might be, even if his

intention were not to search for it, at least

arouses our curiousity, if not our admiration.

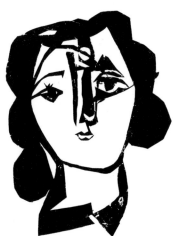

I do not seek.

I find.

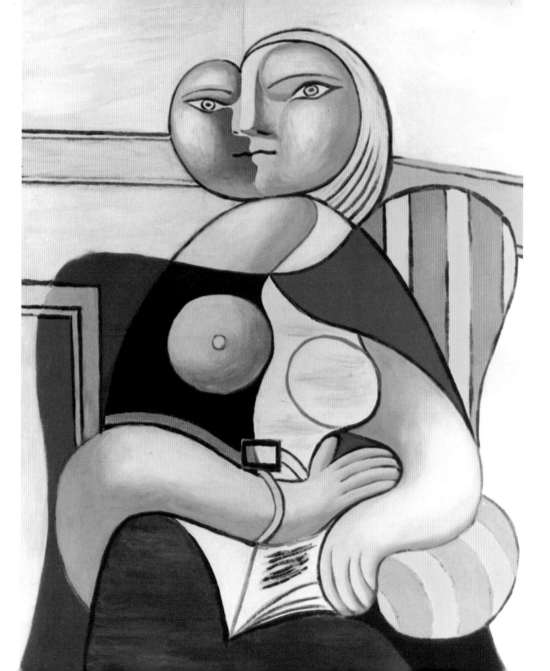

33

*Y*ou see, for me a painting is a dramatic action in the course of which reality finds itself split apart. For me, that dramatic action takes precedence over all other considerations. The pure plastic act is only secondary as far as I'm concerned. What counts is the drama of that plastic act, the moment at which the universe comes out of itself and meets its own destruction.

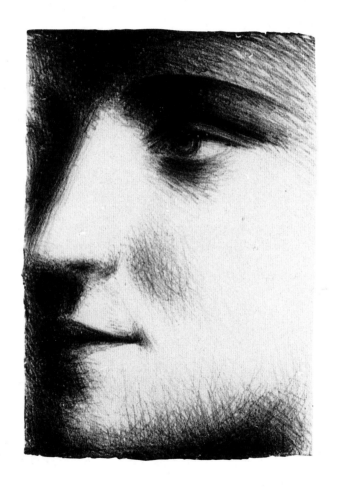

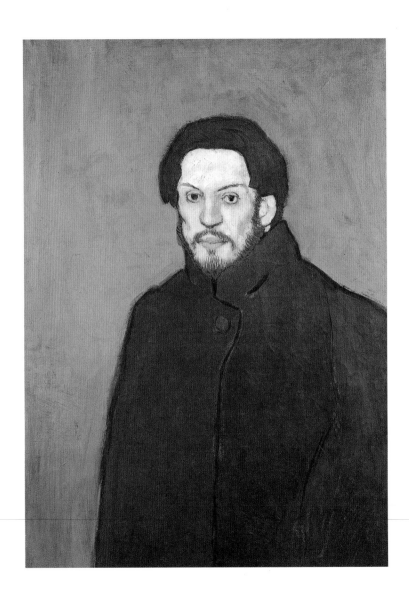

36

*W*hen you have something to say, to express, any form of submission becomes unbearable in the long

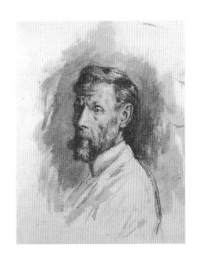

run. You have to have the courage of your vocation and the courage to live by that vocation. The "second profession" is a trap! I was often penniless myself, but I always resisted any temptation to live by any means other than my painting.

*I*t is my wish at this time

to remind you that I have

always believed, and still

believe, that artists who live

and work with spiritual

values cannot and should

not remain indifferent to

a conflict in which the

highest values of humanity

and civilization are at stake.

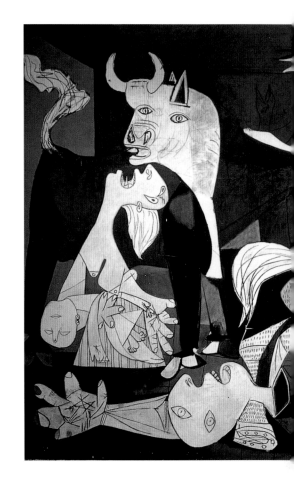

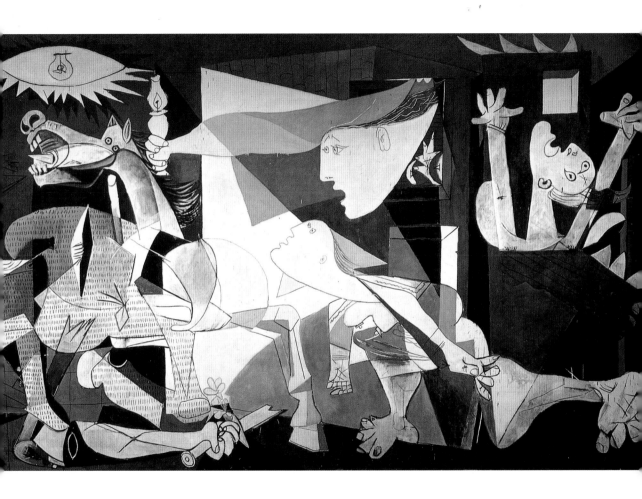

*N*o, painting is not done to decorate apartments.
It is an instrument of war.

*A*s for the gentle dove,
what a myth that is! There's
no crueller animal. I had
some here, and they pecked
a poor little pigeon to death
because they didn't like it.
They pecked its eyes out,
then pulled it to pieces.
It was horrible. How's that
for a symbol of Peace?

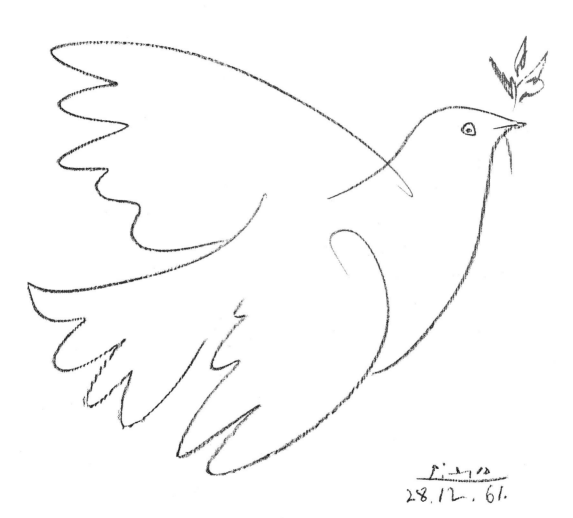

41

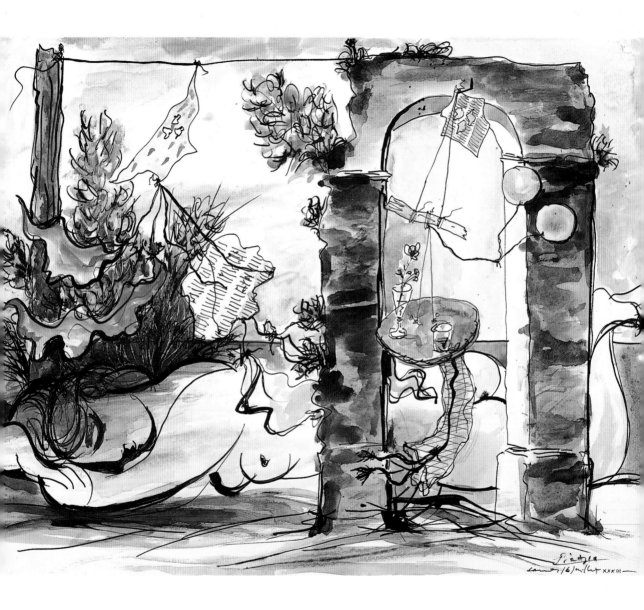

I love what belongs to me, yet at the same time
I have a strong urge to destroy. It's the same with love.

*W*hat I want is to be able to live
like a poor man with plenty of money.

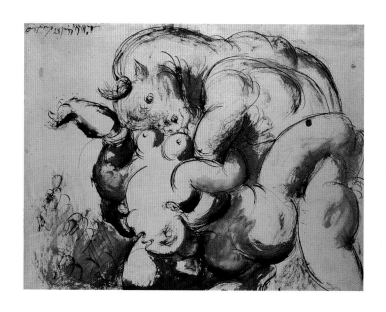

*O*ne can never be careful enough when dealing with the lives of other people. Once, when I was a boy, I saw a spider about to kill a wasp which was caught in its web. Oh, I said to myself, that horrible spider is going to hurt the poor wasp. So I took a large stone . . . and then discovered to my horror that I had killed both of them.

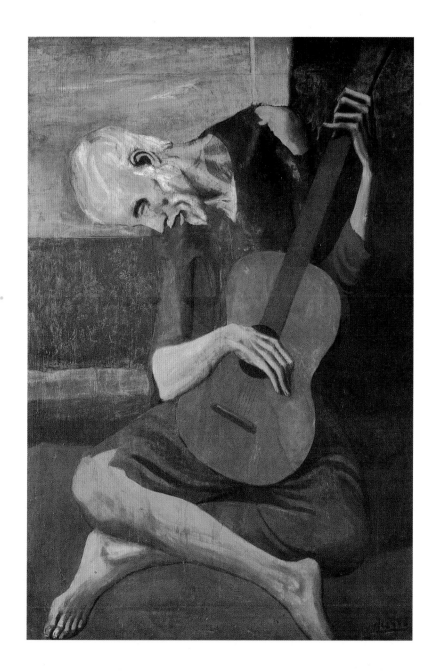

45

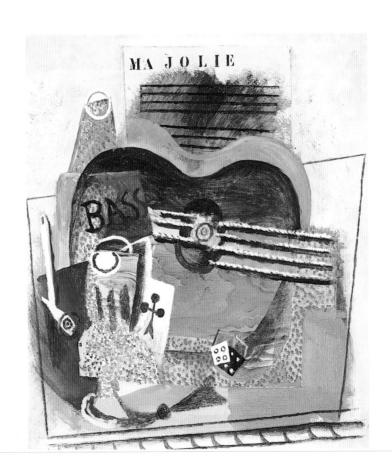

*I*t is my misfortune—and probably my delight—to use things as my passions tell me. . . . I put all the things I like into my pictures. The things—so much the worse for them; they just have to put up with it.

I am not a squanderer. I have what I have because I keep it and not because I save it. Why should I throw away that which was kind enough to reach my hands?

When I paint my object is to show what I have found and not what I am looking for. In art intentions are not sufficient and, as we say in Spanish: love must be proved by facts and not by reasons. What one does is what counts and not what one had the intention of doing.

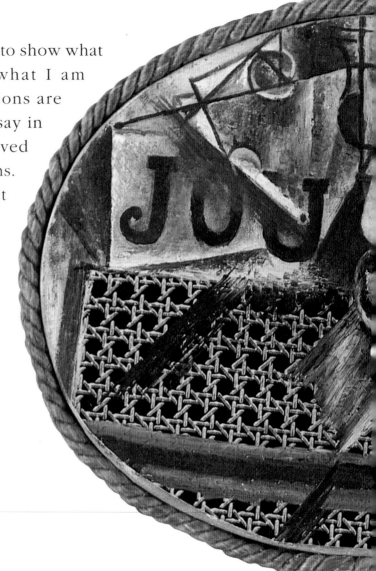

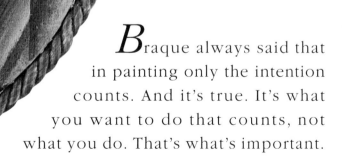

49

*B*raque always said that
in painting only the intention
counts. And it's true. It's what
you want to do that counts, not
what you do. That's what's important.

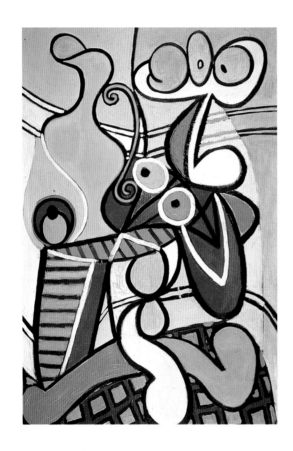

When you begin a picture, you often make some pretty discoveries. You must be on guard against these. Destroy the thing, do it over several times. In each destroying of a beautiful discovery, the artist does not really suppress it, but rather transforms it, condenses it, makes it more substantial. What comes out in the end is the result of discarded finds. Otherwise, you become your own connoisseur. I sell myself nothing.

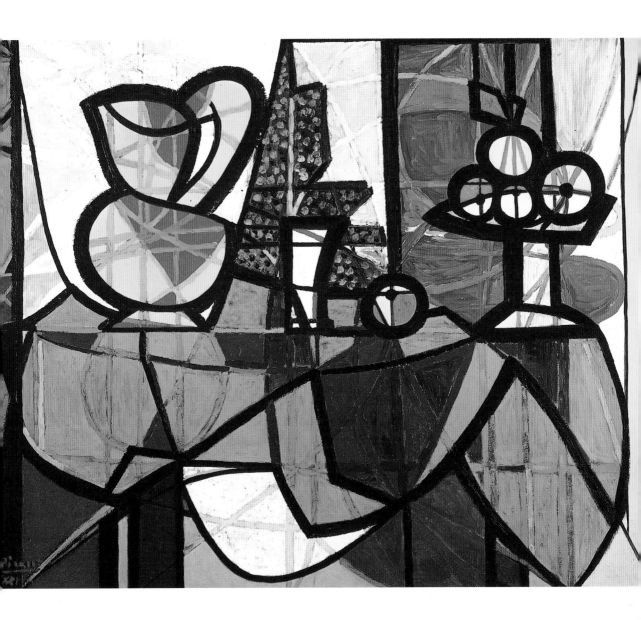

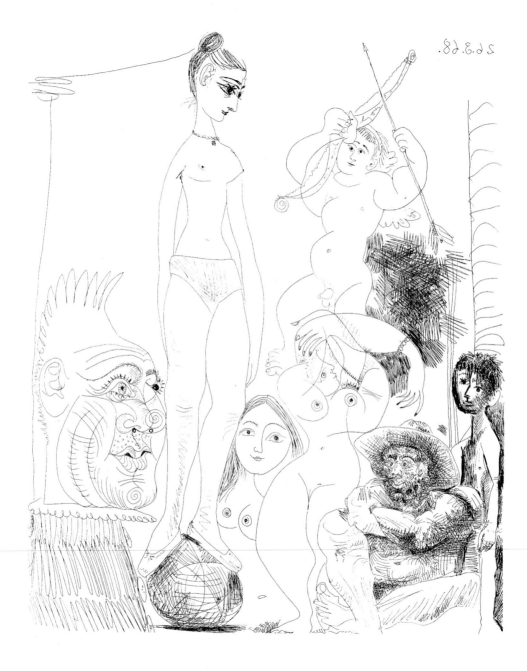

52

26.3.68.

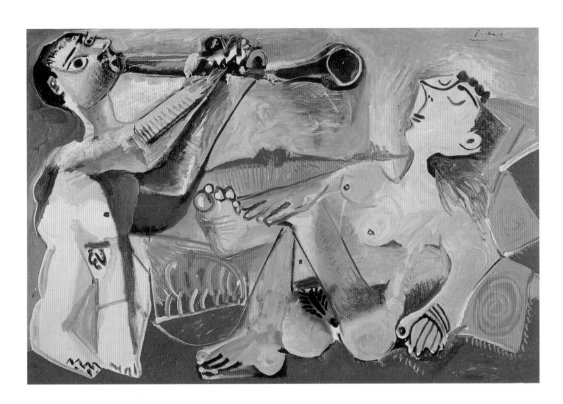

53

When there's anything to steal, I steal.

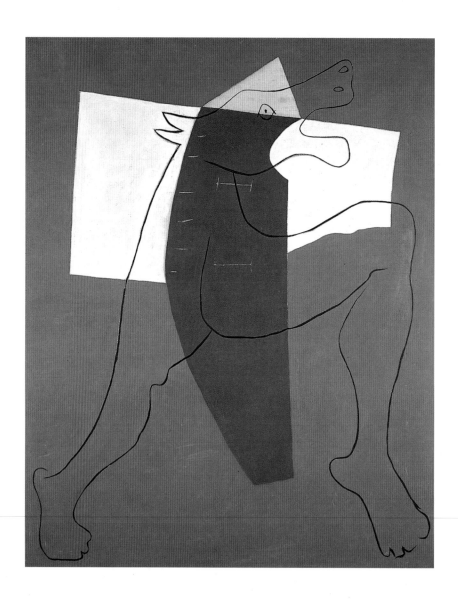

54

*F*orcing yourself to use restricted means is the sort of restraint that liberates invention. It obliges you to make a kind of progress that you can't even imagine in advance.

*Y*ou know, it has happened more than once that someone has called to fetch a drawing that I had promised him and, although it was done, I couldn't find it. So to put things right I would go out of the room "to look for it," and while I was away I would do another one just like it. They never knew the difference.

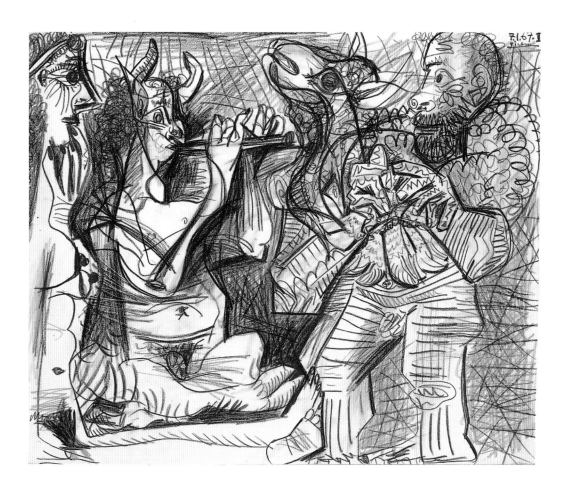

*R*epeatedly I am

asked to explain how

my painting evolved.

To me there is no

past or future in art.

If a work of art cannot

live always in the

present it must not be

considered at all.

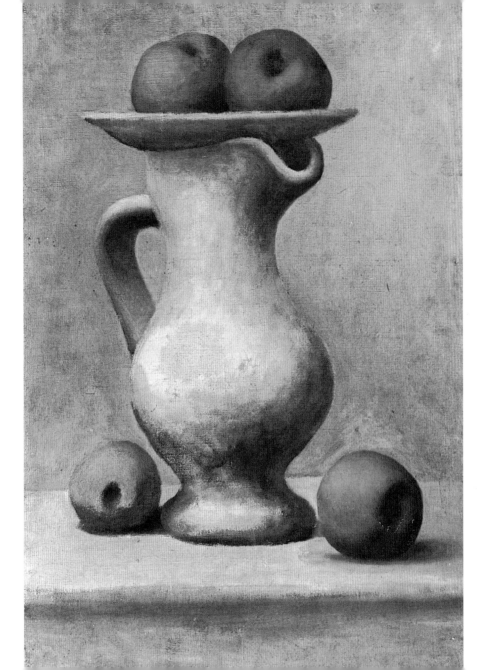

I'm always saying to myself: "That's not right yet. You can do better." It's rare when I can prevent myself from taking a thing up again . . . x number of times, the same thing. Sometimes, it becomes an absolute obsession. But for that matter, why would anyone work, if not for that? To express the same thing, but express it better. It's always necessary to seek for perfection. Obviously, for us, this word no longer has the same meaning. To me, it means: from one canvas to the next, always go further, further . . .

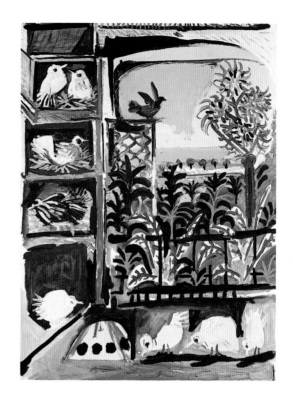

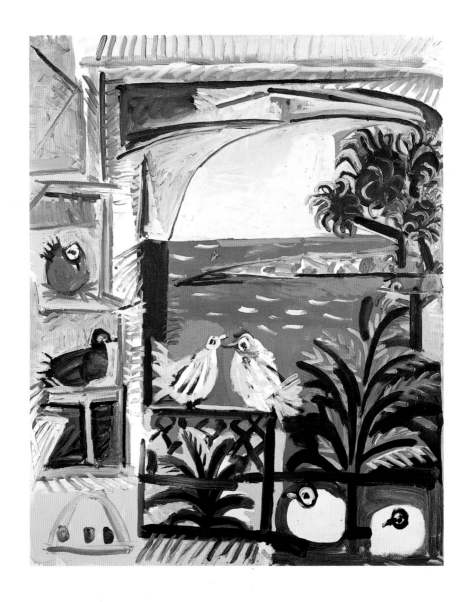

61

62

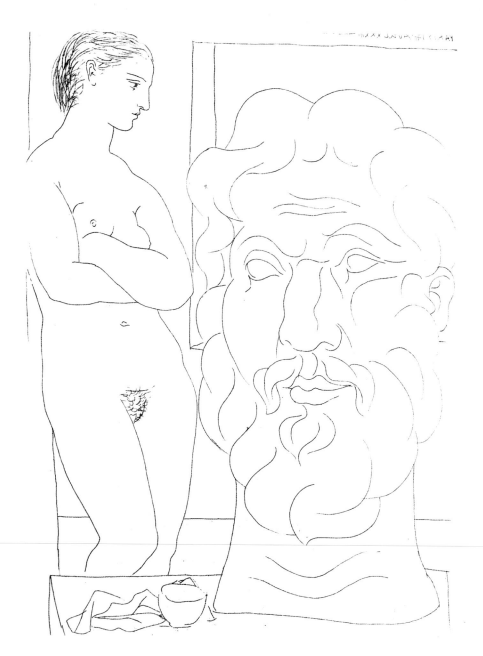

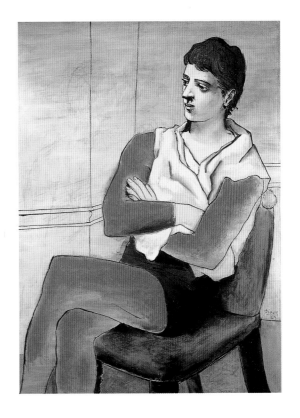

*H*ave you ever seen a finished picture? A picture or anything else? Woe unto you the day it is said that you are finished! To finish a work? To finish a picture? What nonsense! To finish it means to be through with it, to kill it, to rid it of its soul, to give it its final blow: the most unfortunate one for the painter as well as for the picture.

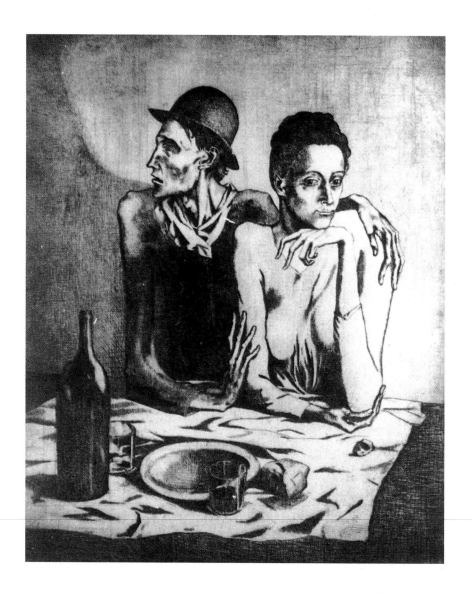

*A*nything of great value—creation, a new idea— carries its shadow zone with it. You have to accept it that way. Otherwise there is only the stagnation of inaction. But every action has an implicit share of negativity. There is no escaping it. Every positive value has its price in negative terms and you never see anything very great which is not, at the same time, horrible in some respect.

The genius of Einstein leads to Hiroshima.

I'm no pessimist, I don't loathe art, because I couldn't live without devoting all my time to it. I love it as the only end of my life. Everything I do connected with it gives me intense pleasure. But still, I don't see why the whole world should be taken up with art, demand its credentials, and on that subject give free rein to its own stupidity. Museums are just a lot of lies, and the people who make art their business are mostly imposters.

A painter paints to unload himself of feelings and visions. People seize on painting to cover up their nakedness. They get what they can wherever they can. In the end I don't believe they get anything at all. They've simply cut a coat to the measure of their own ignorance.

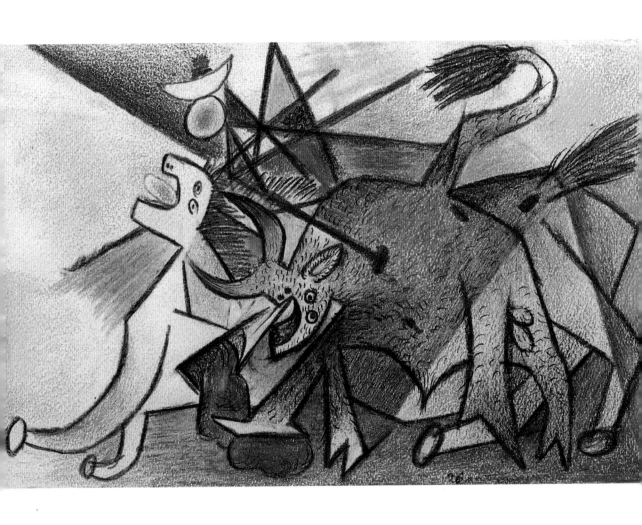

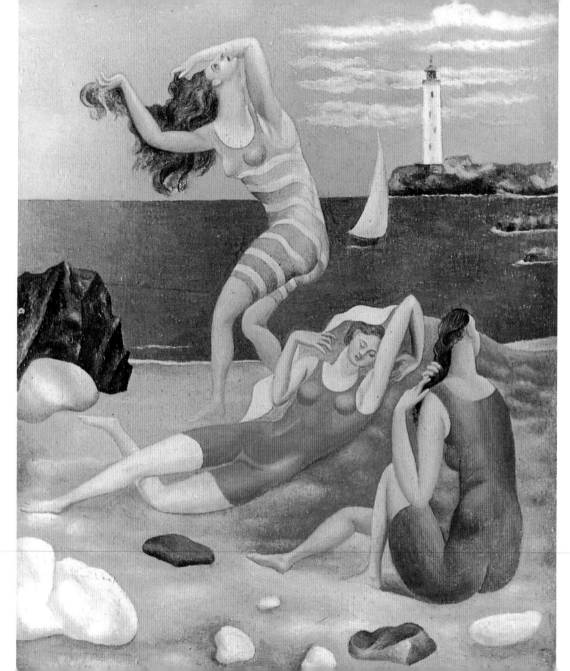

68

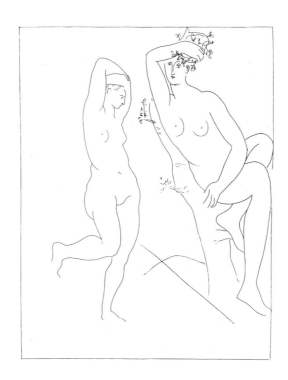

*Y*ou can try anything in painting. You even have a right to.
Provided you never do it again.

*P*ainting is stronger than I am.
It makes me do what it wants.

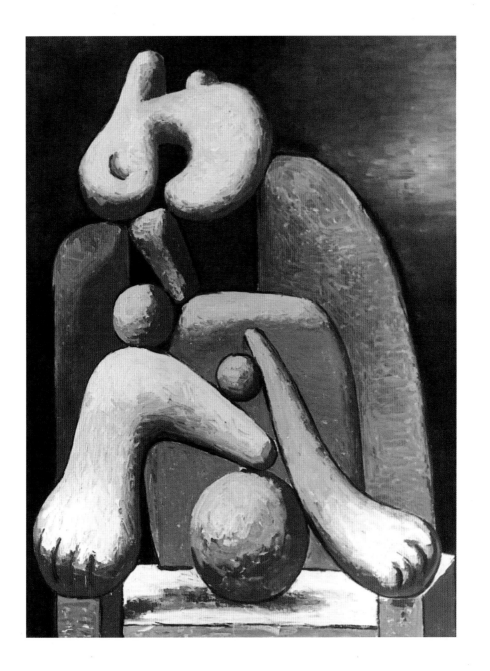

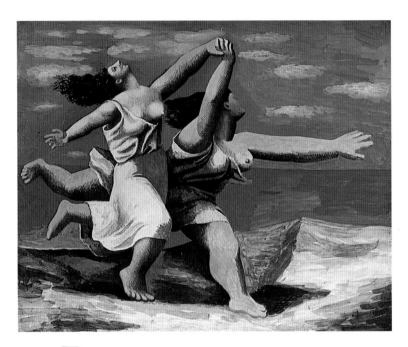

*P*ainters should have their eyes put out
like goldfinches to make them sing better.

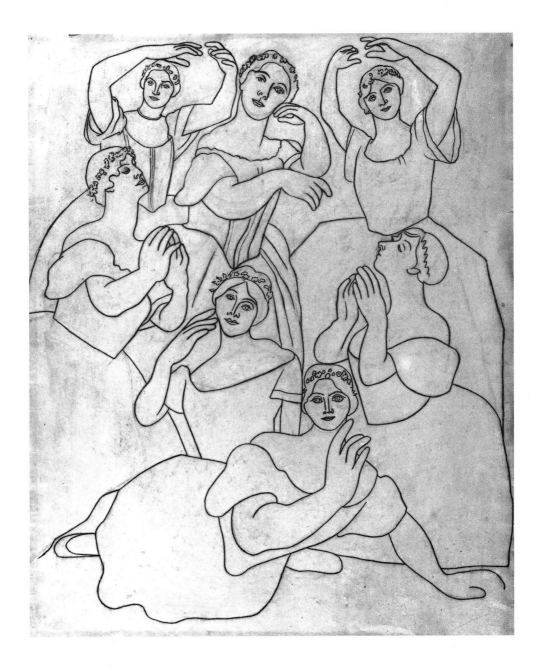

73

*H*ow can you expect an onlooker to live a picture of mine as I lived it? A picture comes to me from miles away: who is to say from how far away I sensed it, saw it, painted it; and yet the next day I can't see what I've done myself. How can anyone enter into my dreams, my instincts, my desires, my thoughts, which have taken a long time to mature and to come out into the daylight, and above all grasp from them what I have been about—perhaps against my own will?

74

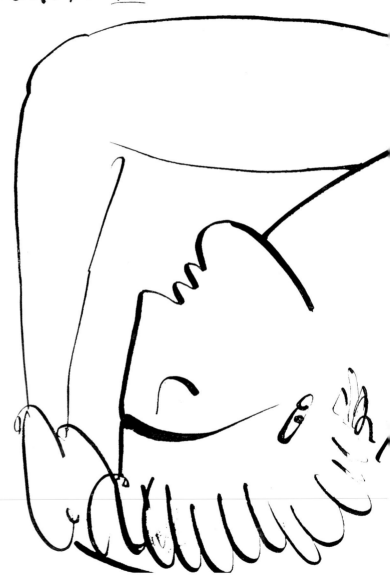

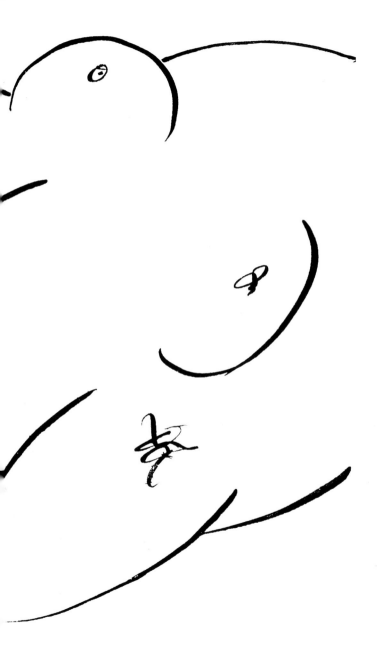

People don't realize
what they have when
they own a picture by me.
Each picture is a phial
with my blood. That is
what has gone into it.

75

*M*atisse makes a
drawing, then he makes a
copy of it. He recopies it
five times, ten times,
always clarifying the line.
He's convinced that the
last, the most stripped
down, is the best, the
purest, the definitive one;
and in fact, most of the
time, it was the first. In
drawing, nothing is better
than the first attempt.

*D*rawing is no joke. There is something very
serious and mysterious about the fact that one can
represent a living human being with line alone and
create not only his likeness but, in addition, an
image of how he really is. That's the marvel!

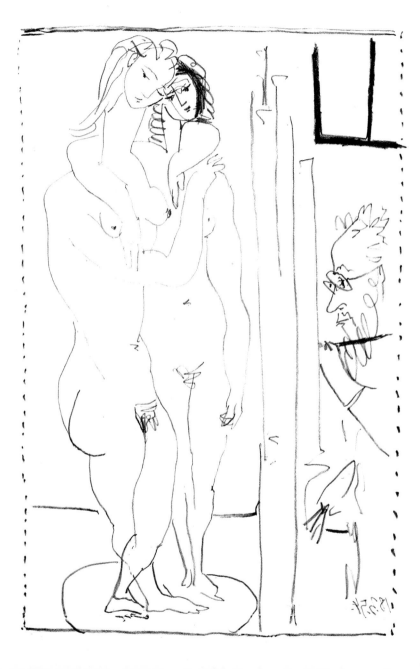

What *is* beauty, anyway?

There's no such thing.

I never *appreciate*, any more than I *like*.

I love or I hate.

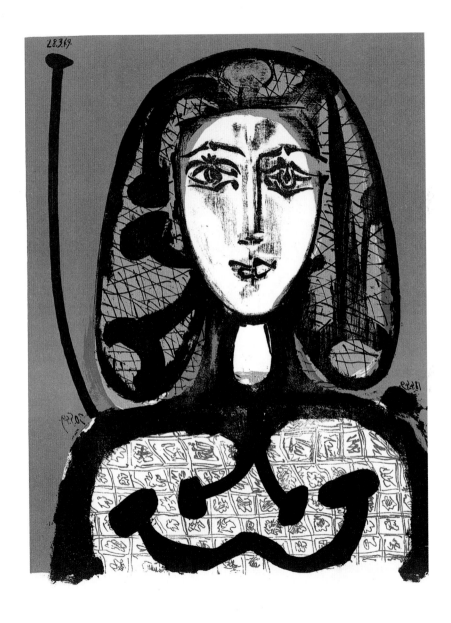

79

*Y*ou know, it's like being a peddler.

"You want two breasts?

Well, here you are—two breasts."

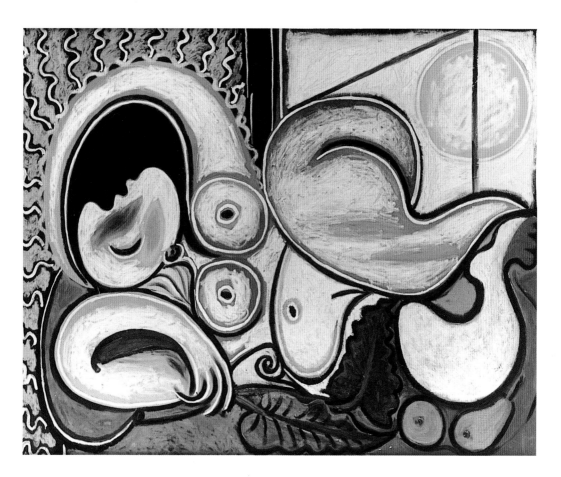

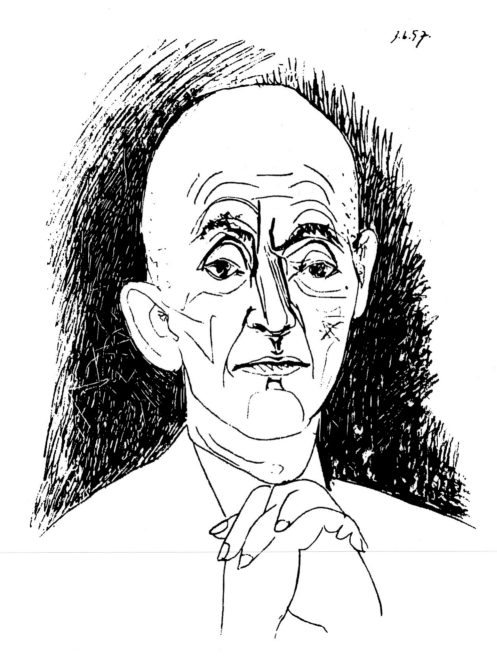

82

1.6.57.

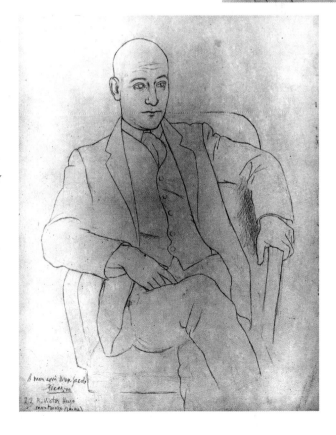

Max Jacob once asked me why I was so nice with people who didn't really matter and so hard on my friends. I told him I didn't care about the first group, but since I cared very much about my friends, it seemed to me I ought to put our friendship to the test every once in a while, just to make sure it was as strong as it needed to be.

83

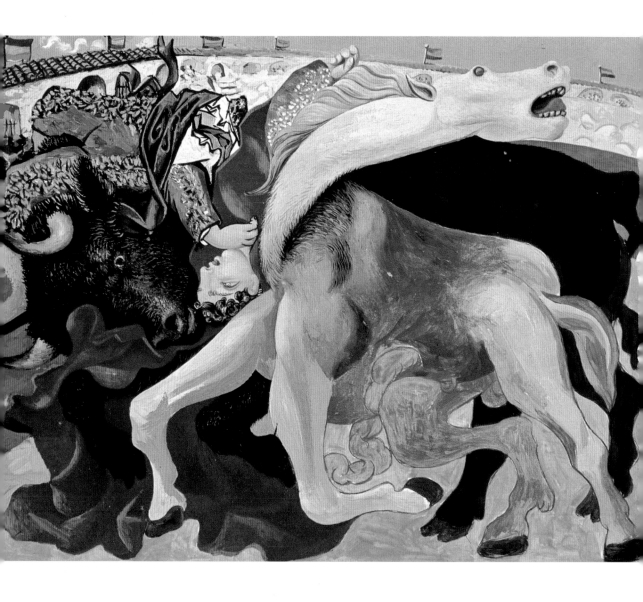

What's the use of disguises and artificialities in a work of art? What counts is what is spontaneous, impulsive. That is the truthful truth. What we impose upon ourselves does not emanate from ourselves.

86

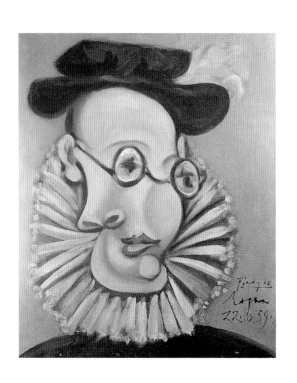

Picasso: There's nothing extraordinary about that pair of shoes but somehow or other I like them. One of these days I'm going to go in and see if they fit me. . . .

Sabartés: Why not now?

Picasso: I'm not in any hurry. Let it go for some day when we get out a little earlier. You know I don't need them right away.

Sabartés: As long as they appeal to you what harm would there be in asking?

Picasso: Of course there would be some harm! If we went in it would take a lot of time. They'd start a conversation, and then every time we went by we'd have to greet them. You know I don't mind this; but after two or three months we'd get to be friends, and then I'd have to worry about the health of the grandfather, the father, the baby . . . and on top of it all I'd have to take the shoes.

I have less and less time, and yet I have more and more to say,

and what I have to say is, increasingly, something about what

goes on in the movement of my thought. I've reached the

moment, you see, when the movement of my thought interests

me more than the thought itself.

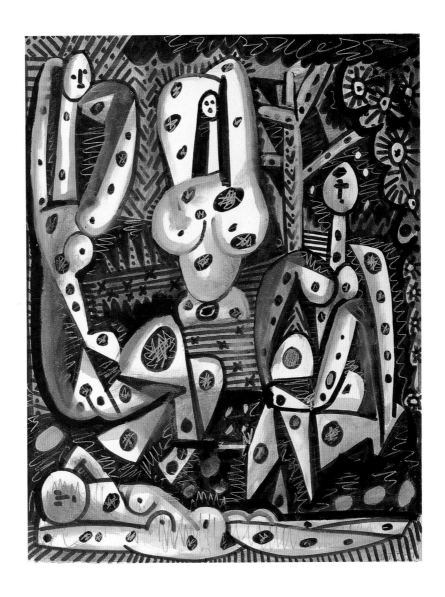

90

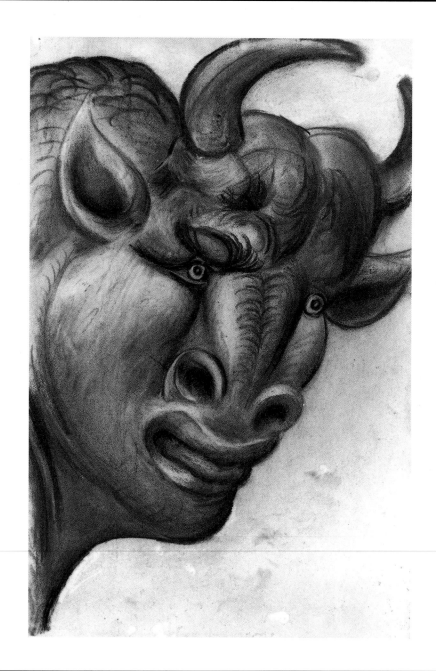

*Y*ou mustn't always believe what I say. Questions tempt you to tell lies, particularly when there is no answer.

NOTES

For the most comprehensive treatment of Pablo Picasso's ideas and thoughts see *Picasso On Art: A Selection of Views*, edited by Dore Ashton and published by Viking Penguin in 1972.

1 Picasso's response to Gilot's comment that if he had not been a painter, he would probably have been known as a philosopher. From 1944. Françoise Gilot and Carlton Lake, *Life with Picasso*, McGraw-Hill, New York, 1964.

6 (left column) A comment Picasso made during a visit by Penrose to the artist's apartment in the rue la Boétie in Paris. Penrose happened to notice that a large painting by Renoir hanging over the fireplace was crooked. No date. Roland Penrose, *Picasso, His Life and Work*, 3rd edition, University of California Press, Berkeley, 1981.

(right column) Hélène Parmelin, *Picasso Plain*, translated from the French by Humphrey Hare, St. Martin's Press, New York, 1963.

7 (left column) Parmelin, *Picasso Plain*.

(right column) Parmelin, *Picasso Plain*.

8 From a conversation with Christian Zervos in 1935. Picasso informally approved Zervos's notes of the artist's remarks, and these were subsequently published under the title "Conversation avec Picasso" in *Cahiers d'Art*, vol. 10, no. 10, 1935. The English version is based on a translation by Myfanwy Evans. Alfred H. Barr, Jr., *Picasso: Fifty Years of His Art*, The Museum of Modern Art, New York, 1946.

11 Statement made in 1946. Gilot, *Life with Picasso*.

12 From a conversation with Christian Zervos in 1935. Barr, *Picasso: Fifty Years of His Art*.

15 From a statement made in Spanish to Marius de Zayas in 1923. Picasso approved de Zayas's manuscript before it was translated into English and published under the title "Picasso Speaks" in *The Arts*, New York, May 1923. Barr, *Picasso: Fifty Years of His Art*.

16 From a statement made to Marius de Zayas in 1923. Barr, *Picasso: Fifty Years of His Art*.

18 Statement made in 1938. Jaime Sabartés, *Picasso: An Intimate Portrait*, translated from the Spanish by Angel Flores, Prentice-Hall, New York, 1948.

20 Sabartés recalled that, at the end of many an evening, Picasso would jokingly prod him with half-serious questions in order to prolong the conversation. After 1935. Sabartés, *Picasso: An Intimate Portrait*.

23 (top) Statement made in 1944. Gilot, *Life with Picasso*.

(bottom) Statement made after 1940. Geneviève Laporte, *Sunshine At Midnight: Memories of Picasso and Cocteau*, translated by Douglas Cooper, Macmillan, New York, 1975.

24 (top) A remark on the subject of work. No date. Hélène Parmelin, *Picasso Says*, translated by Christine Trollope, George Allen and Unwin, London, 1969.

(bottom) A remark on the subject of picture dealing. No date. Gilot, *Life with Picasso*.

26 No date. Parmelin, *Picasso Says*.

29 (top) An angry response to a publisher who had dismissed a sculpture by Picasso as an "object." From 1943. Brassaï, *Picasso & Company*, translated from the French by Francis Price, Doubleday, New York, 1966.

(bottom) Statement made in 1944. Gilot, *Life with Picasso*.

31 From a statement made to Marius de Zayas in 1923. Barr, *Picasso: Fifty Years of His Art*.

32 One of Picasso's most famous and oft-quoted remarks. Gilot, in *Life with Picasso*, said that the artist also once offered: "Since everybody is so fond of quoting that remark of mine, 'I don't seek; I find,' I'll give you a new one to put in circulation: 'I don't give; I take.'" Hélène Parmelin, *Picasso: Women*, translated from the French by Humphrey Hare, Editions Cercle d'Art, Paris, and Harry N. Abrams, Amsterdam, 1964.

92

34 Statement made in 1944. Gilot, *Life with Picasso*.

37 Statement made in 1944. Brassaï, *Picasso & Company*.

38 From a statement published in the *New York Times*, December 19, 1937, on the occasion of the American Artists' Congress held in New York. Barr, *Picasso: Fifty Years of His Art*.

39 No date. Barr, *Picasso: Fifty Years of His Art*.

40 Picasso made this remark after Louis Aragon chose the artist's drawing of what Aragon thought to be a dove (it was actually a pigeon) for the poster commemorating the Peace Conference in Paris, April 1949. Laporte, *Sunshine At Midnight*.

43 (top) No date. Laporte, *Sunshine At Midnight*.

(bottom) No date. Daniel-Henry Kahnweiler, with Francis Crémieux, *My Galleries and Painters*, translated from the French by Helen Weaver, Viking Press, New York, 1971.

44 Statement made after 1935. Laporte, *Sunshine At Midnight*.

47 (top) From a conversation with Christian Zervos in 1935. Barr, *Picasso: Fifty Years of His Art*.

(bottom) Picasso offered this remark in defense of one of his most celebrated traits: his penchant for accumulating things and leaving them freely scattered about his dwellings. No date. Sabartés, *Picasso: An Intimate Portrait*.

48 From a statement made to Marius de Zayas in 1923. Barr, *Picasso: Fifty Years of His Art*.

49 No date. Parmelin, *Picasso Says*.

50 From a conversation with Christian Zervos in 1935. Barr, *Picasso: Fifty Years of His Art*.

53 No date. Gilot, *Life with Picasso*.

55 Statement made in 1944. Gilot, *Life with Picasso*.

56 No date. Rosamond Bernier, *Matisse, Picasso, Miró: As I Knew Them*, Alfred A. Knopf, New York, 1991.

58 From a statement made to Marius de Zayas in 1923. Barr, *Picasso: Fifty Years of His Art*.

60 Picasso agreed with the photographer's desire to redo some pictures. From 1943. Brassaï, *Picasso & Company*.

63 No date. Sabartés, *Picasso: An Intimate Portrait*.

65 Statement made in 1946. Gilot, *Life with Picasso*.

66 (left) From a conversation with Christian Zervos in 1935. Barr, *Picasso: Fifty Years of His Art*.

(right) From a conversation with Christian Zervos in 1935. Barr, *Picasso: Fifty Years of His Art*.

69 No date. Parmelin, *Picasso Says*.

70 No date. Parmelin, *Picasso: Women*.

72 No date. Roland Penrose, *The Eye of Picasso*, A Mentor-Unesco Art Book, New American Library, New York, 1967.

74 From a conversation with Christian Zervos in 1935. Barr, *Picasso: Fifty Years of His Art*.

75 Statement made in 1954. Penrose, *Picasso, His Life and Work*.

93

76 (top) Statement made in 1943. Brassaï, *Picasso & Company*.

(bottom) No date. Laporte, *Sunshine At Midnight*.

78 Statement made about 1946. Gilot, *Life with Picasso*.

80 A remark Picasso made to a fellow painter. No date. Parmelin, *Picasso: Women*.

83 Statement made in 1947. Gilot, *Life with Picasso*.

85 Statement made in 1938. Sabartés, *Picasso: An Intimate Portrait*.

87 Sabartés recalled that in Royan, between 1939 and 1940, while passing a certain shoemaker on their customary walks, Picasso would invariably stop and comment on the same pair of shoes. Sabartés, *Picasso: An Intimate Portrait*.

88 Statement made in 1946. Gilot, *Life with Picasso*.

91 No date. Penrose, *Picasso, His Life and Work*.

96 No date. Parmelin, *Picasso Says*.

LIST OF PLATES

1 *Portrait of an Adolescent Dressed as a Pierrot* (1922)
Gouache and watercolor,
11.8 x 10.5 cm
Musée Picasso, Paris

2 *Les Demoiselles d'Avignon* (1907)
Oil on canvas, 243.9 x 233.7 cm
The Museum of Modern Art,
New York

5 *Self-portrait* (1917-1919)
Pencil and charcoal, 64 x 49.5 cm
Musée Picasso, Paris

9 *Flowers* (1901)
Oil on canvas, 65 x 49 cm
The Tate Gallery, London

10 *Seated Woman* (1909-1910)
Oil on canvas, 100 x 81 cm
Van Abbemuseum, Eindhoven

13 *The Two Saltimbanques* (1901)
Oil on canvas, 73 x 60 cm
The State Hermitage Museum,
Saint Petersburg

14 *First Communion* (1895-1896)
Oil on canvas, 166 x 118 cm
Museu Picasso, Barcelona

15 *La Vie* (1903)
Oil on canvas, 196.5 x 128.5 cm
The Cleveland Museum of Art

17 *Nude in a Garden* (1934)
Oil on canvas, 162 x 130 cm
Musée Picasso, Paris

19 *Two Women at a Bar* (1902)
Oil on canvas, 80 x 91.4 cm
Hiroshima Museum of Art

20 *Sculptor and Model with Statue of Centaur Kissing a Girl* (1933)
Etching from the *Vollard Suite*,
19 x 26 cm

21 *The Flute Player* (1946)
Oil-based paint and charcoal
on ochre vellum, 66 x 51 cm
Musée Picasso, Antibes

22 *Figures by the Sea* (1931)
Oil on canvas, 130.5 x 195.5 cm
Musée Picasso, Paris

24 *Olga with a Hat with a Feather* (1920)
Pencil on charcoal outlines,
61 x 48.5 cm
Musée Picasso, Paris

25 *Harlequin with Mirror* (1923)
Oil on canvas, 100 x 81 cm
Thyssen-Bornemisza Museum,
Madrid

27 *Goat Skull, Bottle, and Candle* (1952)
Oil on canvas, 89 x 116 cm
Musée Picasso, Paris

28 *Bottle of Pernod and a Glass* (1912)
Oil on canvas, 45.5 x 32.5 cm
The State Hermitage Museum,
Saint Petersburg

30 *The Reading of the Letter* (1921)
Oil on canvas, 184 x 105 cm
Musée Picasso, Paris

31 *Head of a Woman* (1945)
Lithograph, 34 x 26 cm

33 *Reading* (1932)
Oil on canvas, 130 x 97 cm
Musée Picasso, Paris

35 *Visage* (1928)
Lithograph, 20.4 x 14.2 cm
The Museum of Modern Art,
New York

36 *Self-portrait* (1901)
Oil on canvas, 80 x 60 cm
Musée Picasso, Paris

37 *Portrait of José Ruiz Blasco, the Artist's Father* (1896)
Watercolor, 25.5 x 17.8 cm
Museu Picasso, Barcelona

38-39 *Guernica* (1937)
Oil on canvas, 349.3 x 776.6 cm
Queen Sofia Art Center, Madrid

41 *Dove* from the poster for the
National Peace Congress held in
Issy-Les-Moulineaux in May 1962
Photolithograph, poster
100 x 64.5 cm

42 *Nude* (1933)
Watercolor and India ink on paper
mounted on board
Private Collection

44 *Minotaur Ravishing a Woman* (1933)
Pen, India ink, and tinted wash,
47 x 62 cm
Musée Picasso, Paris

45 *The Old Guitarist* (1903)
Oil on panel, 122.9 x 82.6 cm
The Art Institute of Chicago
Helen Birch Bartlett Memorial
Collection

46 *"Ma Jolie"* (1914)
Oil on canvas, 45 x 40 cm
Private Collection

48-49 *Still Life with Chair Caning* (1912)
Collage of oil, oilcloth, and paper on
canvas, framed with rope,
27 x 35 cm (oval)
Musée Picasso, Paris

50 *Still Life on a Pedestal Table* (1931)
Oil on canvas, 194 x 130 cm
Musée Picasso, Paris

51 *Pitcher and Bowl of Fruit* (1931)
Oil on canvas, 130 x 162 cm
The Museum of Modern Art,
New York

52 *347 Series: No. 9* (1968)
Etching, 42.5 x 34.5 cm

53 *The Serenade* (1965)
Oil on canvas, 130 x 195 cm
Private Collection

54 *Minotaur* (1928)
Oil on canvas, 161.9 x 130.2 cm
Musée Picasso, Paris

57 *Man with a Lamb, Musical Faun,
and Seated Nude* (1967)
Colored pencil, 50 x 61 cm

59 *Still Life with Pitcher and Apples*
(1919)
Oil on canvas, 65 x 43.5 cm
Musée Picasso, Paris

60 *The Pigeons* (1957)
Oil on canvas, 130 x 97 cm
Museu Picasso, Barcelona

61 *The Pigeons* (1957)
Oil on canvas, 100 x 81 cm
Museu Picasso, Barcelona

62 *Model and Sculptured Head* (1933)
Etching from the *Vollard Suite*,
26.3 x 19 cm

63 *Saltimbanque with Arms Crossed*
(1923)
Oil on canvas, 130 x 97 cm
Private Collection

64 *A Frugal Repast* (1904)
Etching, 46.4 x 37.5 cm
Musée Picasso, Paris

67 *Bullfight* (1935)
Colored crayons, pencil, and
India ink, 17.2 x 25.8 cm
Musée Picasso, Paris

68 *The Bathers* (1918)
Oil on canvas, 26.3 x 21.7 cm
Musée Picasso, Paris

69 *Two Nudes in a Tree* (1931)
Etching, 37.5 x 29.8 cm

71 *Woman in a Red Armchair* (1932)
Oil on canvas, 130.2 x 97 cm
Musée Picasso, Paris

72 *Two Women Running on
the Beach* (1922)
Gouache on wood, 32.5 x 41.1 cm
Musée Picasso, Paris

73 *Seven Dancers, with Olga Kokhlova
in the Foreground* (1919)
Pencil with traces of charcoal,
62.2 x 50 cm
Musée Picasso, Paris

74-75 Study for *The Women of Algiers*,
after Delacroix (1955)
Pen and India ink, 21 x 27 cm
Musée Picasso, Paris

77 *Two Nudes Posing* (1954)
Lithograph, 65.1 x 49.8 cm

79 *Woman with Green Hair* (1956)
Lithograph, 66 x 50 cm
Musée Picasso, Antibes

81 *Sleeping Nude* (1932)
Oil on canvas, 130 x 161 cm
Musée Picasso, Paris

82 *Portrait of D. H. Kahnweiler III* (1957)
Lithograph, 64 x 49 cm

83 (top) *Portrait of Erik Satie* (1920)

Pencil, 62.3 x 48 cm
Musée Picasso, Paris

(bottom) *Portrait of Max Jacob*
(1916)
Pencil, 32.6 x 25.3 cm

84 *Bullfight: Death of the Toreador*
(1933)
Oil on wood, 31.2 x 40.3 cm
Musée Picasso, Paris

86 *Portrait of Jaime Sabartés* (1939)
Oil on canvas, 45.7 x 38 cm
Museu Picasso, Barcelona

89 *Four Women in a Landscape* (1955)
India ink, colored crayons, and
gouache, 65 x 50.5 cm
Musée Picasso, Paris

90 *Bull's Head* (1933)
Charcoal, 51 x 34 cm
Musée Picasso, Paris

96 *Self-portrait: Yo Picasso* (1901)
Oil on canvas, 73.5 x 60.5 cm
Private Collection

95

PHOTOGRAPHIC CREDITS

Photo © 1992 The Art Institute of
Chicago: 45. Art Resource, New
York: 1, 10, 17, 20, 21, 22, 27, 30, 33,
35, 42, 48-49, 50, 52, 57, 59, 62, 63,
64, 68, 71, 72, 81, 84, 96. Erich
Lessing / Art Resource, New York:
13, 28. Giraudon / Art Resource,
New York: 14, 36, 37, 38-39, 51, 54,
60, 61, 83 (top and bottom), 86.
Hubert Josse / Art Resource, New
York: 53. Jian Chen / Art Resource,
New York: 77. Nimatalah / Art
Resource, New York: 25. Photo ©
R.M.N.: 5, 24, 44, 67, 73, 74-75, 89, 90.
Scala / Art Resource, New York: 2,
15, 19, 46. Tate Gallery / Art
Resource, New York: 9.

96

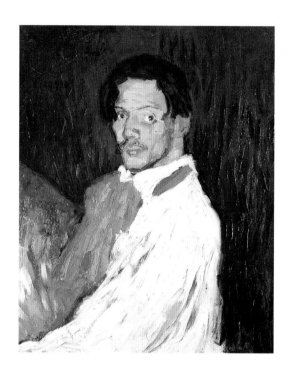

*A*nd in the end when the work is there,
the painter has already gone.